T0195885

FIRM
FOUNDATION

David A. Burgess

authorHOUSE

AuthorHouse™
1663 Liberty Drive
Bloomington, IN 47403
www.authorhouse.com
Phone: 833-262-8899

Published by AuthorHouse 01/06/2022

ISBN: 978-1-6655-3919-7 (sc)
ISBN: 978-1-6655-3918-0 (hc)
ISBN: 978-1-6655-3920-3 (e)

Library of Congress Control Number: 2021924817

Print information available on the last page.

Scripture quotations marked "KJV" are taken from the Holy Bible, King James Version (Public Domain).

This book is printed on acid-free paper.

CONTENTS

PREFACE

When I first came to the saving knowledge of Jesus Christ, I did not know where to start in the word of God, so I began seeking the Lord for direction on what and how to study. Some of the things He showed me were salvation, redemption, faith, covenant, Holy Spirit, and Jesus the Christ. And to prayerfully meditate on the Word of God, so that the Holy Spirit can illuminate the Word and give revelation.

After years of studying the Word of God and applying its life-changing principles to the circumstances that came to me in life, I have learned what it means to walk by faith and not by sight. Now today I know that the Word of God is true and that it works. The Word of God has the ability to change life situations when one lives, acts according to, and does what it says. No matter where you are in life, the Word of the Lord can change you.

I pray that this book will serve as a guide to lead you on a journey to success and prosperity in the things of God. This is just to get you exposed to some of the basic teachings of Christianity. I believe you will receive direction in your walk with the Lord.

I encourage you to study faith, Jesus, redemption, salvation, covenant, and the Holy Spirit. Study each chapter in this book diligently. Look up the scripture given at the bottom of the page and apply what you read to your life. By doing the Word, you will be building on a firm foundation for success in every area of life.

CHAPTER 1

THE FOUNDATION OF FAITH

Faith is the most important part of a born-again believer's life. Faith is the foundation of living a victorious life as a Christian. We, as born-again believers, must know in what we trust and in whom we trust. We put our trust in God and His Word (Jesus only). As a believer, you must find out who you are in Christ, the power in the name of Jesus and in His blood, and how to handle God's money. If we truly discover our privileges as born-again believers, we will not accept lack or defeat. The Word of God tells us what God thinks of us and says about us; therefore, we must meditate on the Word until that Word becomes one with us, and we come to the place where, if God said it, that settles it!

David A. Burgess

The Bible says,

> Have faith in God, for verily I say unto
> you, that whosoever shall say unto this
> mountain, be thou removed, and be thou
> cast into the sea; and shall not doubt in his
> heart, but shall believe that those things
> which he saith shall come to pass; he shall
> have whatsoever he saith.[1]

To have faith in God is also to have faith in His
Word (Jesus only). God put His Word before His
name, and He watches over His Word to perform it.[2]
God's Word is forever settled in heaven. The basis of
our faith must be in the Word of God, where we get
the foundation of our faith. Believing, trusting, and
relying on God, we begin to act on what God has
spoken in His Word.

Faith is one of the most important subjects in a
born-again believer's life. We must have our faith

---

[1] Mark 11:23 KJV.
[2] Jeremiah 1:12 KJV.

developed in every arena of life, including the spiritual, the physical, the financial, our career, and the social aspects. In order to prosper and be successful in our walk as Christians, we must ask ourselves the following questions: What is faith? Where does faith come from? How do we get faith?

It would be unjust for God to demand that we have faith and then not give it to us, and God is not unjust.

Faith is putting legs to what we believe in our heart. Faith does not depend on feelings but a belief that God has, can, and will. "Now faith is the substance of things hoped for, the evidence of things not seen."[3] What we believe has to come from the covenant Word of God. The spirit of man, the real you, is the heart. Your mind, will, and emotions must line up with your spirit, as your spirit guides the reasoning faculties. Your spirit, when filled with the Word of God, builds faith.

---

[3] Hebrews 11:1 KJV.

Let's look at Romans 10:9: "if thou shalt confess with thy mouth the Lord Jesus, and shalt believe in thine heart that God hath raised him from the dead, thou shalt be saved."[4] So from this scripture, we see that we are to have faith in Jesus. In the first chapter of the Gospel of John, the first verse states, "In the beginning was the Word, and the Word was with God, and the Word was God." God and His Word are one. Look also at verse 14: "And the Word was made flesh, dwelt among us, (and we beheld His glory, the glory as of the only begotten of the Father), full of grace and truth." Jesus Christ is the Word of God, and the Word of God is our foundation. Our foundation must be on Christ; any foundation other than Christ will not hold the weight of the world. Faith in the integrity of God's Word is our only foundation.

Real faith comes from the Word of God. Faith comes by hearing and hearing by the Word of God. We come to know the Lord Jesus Christ by the hearing of the Word, but it is a gift: "For by grace are ye saved through faith; and that not of yourselves: it is the gift

---

4 Romans 10:9 KJV.

of God" (Ephesians 1:8). The more we hear and act on the Word of God, the more our faith will increase. We will no longer have to think about our faith; we will just trust God for His Word and begin acting on the Word with unqualified faith. The Word must dwell in us. To obtain this kind of faith, we have to meditate and stay in the Word until the Word is increased inside us, causing the effect of the world's issues to decrease outside us. When this happens, you will have all the confidence you need to overcome the world: "For whatsoever is born of God overcometh the world: and this is the victory that overcometh the world, even our faith."[5]

Romans 10:9 tells us "that if thou shalt confess with thy mouth, the Lord Jesus, and shalt believe in thine heart that God hath raised Him from the dead, thou shalt be saved." The mouth plays a very significant role. What we believe in our hearts will come out of our mouths. If the Word does not get in our hearts, it will not come out of our mouths.

---

[5] 1 John 5:4 KJV.

A good man out of the good treasure (deposit) of his heart bringeth forth that which is good; and an evil man out of the evil treasure (deposit) of his heart bringeth forth that which is evil: for of the abundance of the heart his mouth speaketh.[6]

What is in a man's heart in abundance will come to pass, because what is in a man's heart, he will speak. Speaking faith-filled words releases power: "Through faith we understand that the world was framed by the word of God, so that things which are seen were not made of things which do appear."[7]

If we truly have faith, it will come out in the words we speak. Saying what you believe and acting on it according to the Word of God is the spirit of faith.

---

[6] Luke 6:45 KJV.

[7] Hebrews 11:3 KJV.

"We having the same spirit of faith, according as it is written, I believed, and therefore have I spoken; we also believe, and therefore speak."[8]

Your faith is no greater than your confession, and you will possess only what you confess. Faith will never rise higher than the level of your confession.

Jesus said, "Have faith in God, for verily I say unto you, that whosoever shall say unto this mountain, be thou removed, and be thou cast into the sea; and shall not doubt in his heart, but shall believe that those things which he saith shall come to pass; he shall have whatsoever he saith."[9] Real faith will say there is nothing too hard for my God. *Confession* (*Homeologeo*, "I confess") is a word of Greek origin that means that you "agree with" or "say the same thing that God says about you and/or your circumstances."[10] Again,

---

[8] 2 Corinthians 4:13 KJV.

[9] Mark 11:23 KJV.

[10] *Strong's Concordance*. Strong, James. Strong's Exhaustive Concordance of the Bible. Abingdon Press, 1890.

releasing faith-filled words will show what is in you in abundance.

Just quoting scriptures and memorizing them does not qualify as faith. Faith is being fully persuaded in your heart. Your confession should be this: "The Word declares that I am healed, and I thank God for it, and I praise Him for it, because it has already been settled."

One of the hardest things for most Christians is calling those "things which be not as though they were." The Bible says, "before Him whom he believed, God, who quickenth the dead, and calleth those things which be not as though they were."[11] Faith does not go by sight; it goes by the Word of God. It is a believer's duty to lay hold to the promises of God and not move off them. Faith reaches out in the unseen world of the spirit and brings the Word into reality, and our mouth signs for the goods. Now all we have to do is to act on the Word in order to obtain it.

---

[11] Romans 4:17 KJV.

What has to be deep in our spirit is that God is able to perform His Word. Believing in God is not enough; it's *what* you believe about your God. He must become personal, and you must believe He is a Healer, Provider, Counselor, and Rewarder. God the Father's love for us must be in our hearts. We must believe that He has our best interests at heart. This comes only from spending time with the Father and His Word through Jesus: "But without faith it is impossible to please Him: for he that cometh to God must believe that He is, and that He is a rewarder of them that diligently seek Him" (Hebrews 11:6).

Romans 12:3 tells us that every born-again Christian has been dealt the same measure of faith, but our faith must be developed:

> "For I say, through the grace given unto me, to every man that is among you, not to think of himself more highly than he ought to think; but to think soberly,

according as God hath dealt to every man the measure of faith."[12]

We were all given the same measure of faith as the big-time preachers. By rightly dividing the Word of God, we can see that every born-again Christian has faith: "For ye are all the children of God by faith in Christ Jesus."[13]

Most of our problem is the renewing of our mind to the truth that God indwells us.

> I beseech you therefore, brethren, by the mercies of God, that ye present your bodies a living sacrifice, holy, acceptable unto God which is your reasonable service. And be not conformed to this world: but be ye transformed by the renewing of your mind, that ye may prove what is that good, and acceptable, and perfect, will of God.[14]

---

[12] Romans 12:3 KJV

[13] Galatians 3:26 KJV.

[14] Romans 12:1–2 KJV.

Renewing the mind according to the Word of God will transform our old "stinkin' thinkin'" to what God has to say about us and thinks about us. "Stinkin' thinkin'" is a way of thinking that is contrary to the Word of God. The body has to be brought into subjection to the renewed mind, and the renewed mind has to be brought into subjection to the recreated spirit. We must receive the Word of God when it speaks to our hearts for it to work on our behalf. Just like you receive the Word for salvation, you have to receive the Word concerning healing, prosperity, and the baptism of the Holy Spirit the same way—also by faith.

Being in Christ Jesus makes you a new creation.[15] "And be renewed in the spirit of your mind; And that ye put on the new man, which after God is created in righteousness and true holiness."[16] It is in the new birth a man's spirit is completely reborn, and it is the man's responsibility to renew his mind to the Word of God. Righteousness is one of the most vital

---

[15] 2 Corinthians 5:17–21 KJV.

[16] Ephesians 4:23, 24 KJV.

areas in the Christian walk. Without knowledge of righteousness, you will never obtain all that is yours in inheritance.

When a person receives Jesus as Lord of his or her life, he or she is made righteous. By being brought into right standing with God, every believer is given privileges or rights as God's child. Righteousness is what you are and is not relevant to good merit or behavior. However, righteousness will affect the way you live. It is faith in Christ Jesus and His redemptive work at Calvary that brings you into right standing with God. We cannot grow in righteousness, but we can become more righteous conscious. You are a heavenly citizen with the Anointed One and His Anointing, which is Christ. In Christ Jesus, you are entitled to everything in His kingdom. Everything Jesus purchased for us on Calvary we can obtain by faith. So we must take our position and take authority. In order for our faith to develop, righteousness has to be a living reality.

We have discussed some of the scriptures that strengthen our walk of faith, but there are two things that empower faith. Love and patience are also necessary tools we need in order to walk by faith. Faith works by love. "Charity (love) suffereth long, and is kind; charity (love) envieth not; charity (love) vaunteth not itself, is not puffed up."[17] Love is the strongest force in the entire world. Love covers a multitude of sins.[18] The Bible also says, "love never fails."[19] God the Father gave us His Son Jesus, and Jesus can never fail.[20] This is why we must put our trust in the Word (Jesus).

Faith and patience are the power twins. Together, they will produce every time. "Knowing this, that the trying of your faith worketh patience. But let patience have her perfect work, that ye may be perfect and entire, wanting nothing."[21] Without the power

---

[17] 1 Corinthians 13:4 KJV.

[18] 1 Peter 4:8 KJV.

[19] 1 Corinthians 13:8 KJV.

[20] John 3:16 KJV.

[21] James 1:3, 4 KJV.

of patience at work, we will allow our five senses to overwhelm our faith. We, as born-again believers, must not get impatient because we do not see the manifestation of the promise we are believing God for out of His Word. It is important that we understand patience. Patience is being constant or being the same way at all times. Patience guards against doubt and fear. It is always responding to every circumstance of life by the Word of God. Patience says God is always faithful, and there is nothing that faith can't overcome.

Patience will always bring victory in a believer's life. "Cast not away therefore your confidence, which hath great recompense of reward. For ye have need of patience, that, after ye have done the will of God, ye might receive the promise. For yet a little while, and he that shall come will come, and will not tarry. Now the just shall live by faith: but any man draw back, my soul shall have no pleasure in him."[22] Patience, faith, and love are unstoppable when they are at work. Do

---

[22] Hebrews 10:35–38 KJV.

not be moved by feelings; only believe that with God all things are possible.

No matter how small your faith is; faith still works. Faith can be as small as a mustard seed and still produce the desired result. If we mix our faith with the Word of God, it will work every time. "For unto us was the gospel preached, as well as unto them: but the word preached did not profit them, not being mixed with faith in them that heard it."[23] Faith will take some action on our behalf. This is when we must know the Word of God and the voice of God. Many have made the mistake of doing their will and not the Father's will, which results in tremendous failure. If faith is appropriated properly, you will get the desired product, because God's Word will always produce.

James 2:26 says, "For as the body without the spirit is dead, so faith without works is dead also."[24] If we have faith, works will later follow. You will have the heartbeat of the Father. You will understand

---

[23] Hebrews 4:2 KJV.

[24] James 2:26 KJV.

your purpose in the kingdom and your God-given assignment.

> But, beloved, we are persuaded better things of you, and things that accompany salvation, though we thus speak. For God is not unrighteous to forget your work and labour of love, which ye have showed toward his name, in that ye have ministered to the saints, and do minister, and we desire that every one of you do show the same diligence to the full assurance of hope unto the end. That ye be not slothful, but followers of them who through faith and patience inherit the promises.[25]

Real faith is equal to service, good stewardship, and your mouth in line with the Word of God. Real faith is proved when these qualities are evident in your life. Faith requires corresponding action.

---

[25] Hebrews 6:8–12 KJV.

Bishop Hank Furr said,

> Real faith (believing, trusting, relying and acting on God's Word) always produces, that is, faith in God and His Word. We must proceed beyond believing in God to believing God. We must believe every word He has revealed to us in the Bible, that is the foundation of "Faith," the Word! All through the Bible we find God's promises, His directions on how to obtain them and His mercy and grace empowering believers to reach these promises even when they first fail to realize all God has for them. Thanks be to God for His faithful mercy and grace that never gives up on us, even when we do and others do also![26]

Jesus is the author and finisher of our faith. The quality that pleases God must be built on the living

---

[26] Dr. Hank Furr, *Light House Revival Center*, Bulletin, January 25, 2004.

Word of God. As we trust God at His Word and begin to act on His Word, we will walk the victorious life that God's Word promises to produce. We must put our trust in Jesus only and let the Word of God have final authority. Our attitude must be if God said it, it is settled. As we renew our mind to the word of God and begin to speak by faith to call those things that be not as though they were, we will have what we say. A firm foundation is mixing our confession with action to put the force of faith to work.

Find out what the Bible is saying to you and what the Bible is saying about you, and then stand on the Word of God. Do not be moved by your five senses or the opinions of others. As you walk in love and patience, you will see the Word work in your life. Faith always works when we apply it to the covenant Word of God.

CHAPTER 2

JESUS

Jesus as the Christ, the Son of the living God, came and changed the world as the people knew it. His teachings were far above the teachings of the Scribes and Pharisees. The product of Israel's conception of God was the Pharisee. Pharisees were proud, bitter, unkind, arrogant, and self-seeking. Israel had such a false conception of God that they didn't recognize Him when He stood in their midst. John 1:14 says, "And the Word became flesh, and pitched his tent among us. And we gazed upon His glory, a glory as an Only-Begotten from His Father."[27] Jesus only spoke the words of God His Father.

When Christ was born 2,000 years ago, the time was ripe for His coming. The civilization of Greece had rendered a great service in preparing the way

---

[27] John 1:14 KJV.

for Christianity by furnishing it with a worldwide language, the most beautiful, the most flexible, the most expressive the world had ever known.

When Christ appeared, the political power of the world was in Roman hands. Never had peace so generally prevailed, never had life and property been so safe, and never had travel been so easy. However, the most deplorable picture of depraved morals in the entire range of history is presented by the Roman world at the time that Christ was born. In all the world, there was nothing to give hope or relief to darkened humanity. In the midst of this condition of despondency and failure, there was a longing for relief.

The following presents some of the attributes and the authority of His name as referenced by *The Vines Expository Dictionary*.

Jesus
Phil 2:10

10) That at the name of Jesus every knee should bow, of things in heaven, and

things in earth, and things under the earth; (KJV)

Of Hebrew origin [3091]; Jesus (i.e. Jehoshua), the name of our Lord and two (three) other Israelites: Joshua, Jehovah is salvation; is the Savior. It was given to the Son of God Incarnation as His personal name, in obedience to the command of an angel to Joseph, the husband of His Mother, Mary, shortly before He was born.

2424 Iesous (ee-ay-sooce'); Greek[28]

Philippians 2:1–11

(2.) His exaltation: Wherefore God also hath highly exalted Him. His exaltation was the reward of His humiliation. Because He humbled Himself, God

---

[28] W. E. Vine, et al.,John R. Kohlenberger, James A. Swanson, *The Vines Expository Dictionary* (Thomas Nelson, 1996), 333.

exalted Him; and He highly exalted Him, hyperypsose, raised Him to an exceeding height. He exalted His whole person, the human nature as well as the divine; for He is spoken of as being in the form of God as well as in the fashion of man. As it respects the divine nature, it could only be the recognizing of His rights, or the display and appearance of the glory He had with the Father before the world was, not any new acquisition of glory; and so the Father Himself is said to be exalted. But the proper exaltation was of His human nature, which alone seems to be capable of it, though in conjunction with the divine. His exaltation here is made to consist in honor and power. In honor so He had a name above every name, a title of dignity above all the creatures, men and angels. And in power: Every knee must bow to him.

The whole creation must be in subjection to Him: things in heaven, and things in earth, and things under the earth, the inhabitants of heaven and earth, the living and the dead. At the name of Jesus, not at the sound of the word, but the authority of Jesus. And that every tongue should confess that Jesus Christ is Lord. Every nation and language should publicly own the universal empire of the exalted Redeemer, and that all power in heaven and earth is given to Him.[29]

In observing the vast extent of the kingdom of Christ, we see it reaches to heaven and earth and to all the creatures in each, to angels as well as men, and to the dead as well as the living, to the glory of God the Father. It is to the glory of God the Father to confess that Jesus Christ is Lord, for it is His will that all men should honor the Son as they honor the Father. Whatever respect is paid to Christ redounds to

---

[29] Matthew 28:18 KJV.

the honor of the Father. "He who receives Me receives Him who sent Me."

Christ also holds the position of Lord of the universe in His own right, first, because He is the Creator. "All things were made by him: and without him was not anything made that was made."[30] But He is Lord of all for another bids to despoil God's fair creation, until as Paul says, "The whole creation groaneth and travaileth in pain together."[31]

It was prophesied that the Messiah would come from the line of David, the greatest king to have ruled the Hebrew nation, after the flesh.

God became man that He might save man. Nothing is more obvious than the fact that for humanity to survive, it must have a Savior. The wise men of this world, the philosophers, the intellectuals, are preoccupied in devising ways and means for man to save himself. The utter failure of man's best efforts

---

[30] John 1:3 KJV
[31] Romans 8:22 KJV

to become his own Savior are reflected in today's big bailouts and breakdowns and the failure of the very foundation of society.

There is one essential aspect to understanding the mission and teaching of Christ. The hearer must first settle in his or her heart the all-important question of whether Jesus is actually divine or only human, whether He is the Son of God, uniquely the only begotten of the Father, or merely a human. Jesus said, "I am the Son of God," but the proud Pharisees could not accept the revelation.

The first thing that impressed people about Christ when they heard Him was the authority with which He spoke. There was remarkable authority in His voice; at the same time, there was a strange directness about His words that pierced the very hearts and consciences of men. When people heard the famous sermon he preached on the mountain, they were not only struck by the wisdom and simplicity of His words but with the authority with which He spoke.

Many men sought to build their empires by shedding the blood of others. Christ, too, came to establish a kingdom—one that is universal and eternal—though not by killing others but by giving His own life. Christ's kingdom is far greater than man's and is in the hearts of His people. Christ is unique in that He inaugurated His kingdom not by shedding the blood of others but by giving His own blood.

The Old Covenant was written by God through prophets who lived 500 to 1500 years before Christ was born. They prophesied of His coming to earth and of many events in His life. The New Covenant, inspired also of God and written by devout followers of Christ, points again and again to how Christ's life fulfilled these prophecies. Many great men have lived and made their mark on the world, but they all died, and their bones still lie in their graves. Only in one place in the world is there an empty tomb. That is in Jerusalem, at the foot of Calvary where they once laid the Lord Jesus Christ. Christ was the first man who lived on earth and received a resurrected body.

The risen Christ was more than a spirit; He had a real body.

Christ was the only person in the world who was born of the Holy Spirit rather than the will of man. Indeed, the fact is that if Christ were the Son of God, He had to be born of the Holy Spirit. Christ was truly more than a man; He was the only begotten of the Father. The ministry of Jesus was a ministry of deliverance. He did not come to rid the nation of the Romans but to set free the spirits and bodies of men from sin and sickness.

"The Spirit of the Lord God is upon me; because the Lord hath anointed me to preach good tidings unto the meek; He hath sent Me to bind up the brokenhearted, to proclaim liberty to the captives, and the opening of the prison to them that are bound; To proclaim the acceptable year of the Lord, and the day of vengeance of our God; to comfort all that mourn."[32] This prophecy told Him many things. First, He was to receive a special anointing of the Spirit, by

---

[32] Isaiah 61:1–2 KJV.

which He would be given power to perform the work that lay before Him.

The question of who Christ is has been answered in many ways. Some have considered Jesus only as one of those especially gifted individuals who come into the world from time to time. They say He was a man with a unique personality and possessed unusual talents, but He was still only a man. This view has been tenaciously held by a certain school of thought from the days of Christ on down to the present. It has a special hold upon those types of thinkers who commonly go under the name of Unitarians. The Unitarian holds that physical laws of nature are invariable and constant and that all true knowledge is a product of the observation of these physical laws. This view, of course, excludes all miracles and denies the divine inspiration of the Scriptures.

There is a second class of people who look upon Christ as more than human but less than divine. They admit the grandeur of Christ's nature and the excellence and sublimity of His teachings. They exalt Him above the angels but not at the level of a deity.

The Christ could not be born by natural generation. God's first promise of the Christ is given in His conversation with Satan just after man's sin of high treason.

"And I will put enmity between thee and the woman, and between thy seed and her seed: He shall bruise thy head, and thou shalt bruise His heel."[33] The Father God realized that man's need could only be met by the incarnation of His Son. He realized that the Christ could not be born of natural generation, so He gave a prophecy that a woman would give birth to a child independent of natural generation, and that the child would be called "the seed of woman."

"And He said, Hear ye now, O House of David: Is it a small thing for you to weary men, that ye will weary my God also? Therefore the Lord Himself will give you a sign: behold the Virgin shall conceive, and

---

[33] Genesis 3:15 KJV.

bear a son, and shall call his name Immanuel."[34] The child is going to be born of the House of David, and the "Lord Himself will give you a sign." Here He uses the name Adonai; the God of Miracles Himself will show you a miracle, a wonder. Something out of the ordinary is going to take place, and we say, "What is it?"

He says, "The virgin shall conceive and bear a son and his name shall be Immanuel." A virgin was going to give birth to a son in a supernatural way, and she was going to call his name Immanuel (God with us).

"And behold, thou shalt conceive in thy womb, and bring forth a son, and shalt call his name Jesus. He shall be great, and shall be called the Son of the Most High; and the Lord God shall give unto Him the throne of His Father David; and He shall reign over the House of Jacob forever; and of His kingdom there shall be no end."[35]

---

[34] Isaiah 7:13 KJV.

[35] Luke 1:31–36 KJV.

Adam was created, and the rest of the human race was generated by natural processes, but this child who was going to be born was to be "formed" by a special act of divine power. Paul speaks of His birth in the following words: "Who, existing in the form of God, counted not the being on an equality with God a thing to be grasped, but emptied Himself, taking the form of a servant, being made in the likeness of men; and being found in fashion as a man, He humbled Himself, becoming obedient unto death, Yea, the death of the cross."[36] Here is a being with whom God performs a miracle by taking Him out of the Godhead or from the Godhead in heaven and placing Him in the womb of a virgin to be united with flesh by a unique conception.

Seventeen times in the Gospel of John, it is declared that Jesus was sent forth from the Father and came to the Earth and that He again left the earth and went unto the Father. The entire Gospel of John is based upon the fact that Jesus had a previous existence with the Father and that while He was walking the earth,

---

[36] Philippians 2:6–8 KJV.

31

he remembered His experiences in the other world and spoke to the Father of these experiences and also of when He would go back and take up again life with the Father.

"The Word was God." The Christ, who was in fellowship and companionship with God, was God. He possessed the same nature. When the fullness of time had come, God sent forth His Son. When Christ was born two thousand years ago, the time was ripe for His coming. God in His providence had brought about these conditions that the news of redemption might be quickly heralded to the world.

In the entire world, there was nothing to give hope or relief to darkened humanity. In the midst of this condition of despondency and failure, there was a longing for relief. The hope of a Redeemer lay in the very atmosphere of the age.

Today, man still hungers for something more than the same old stuff. Education has not eliminated from man's spirit this hunger. Every modern human religion tries to answer this hunger. Only Jesus can satisfy a man's soul.

> How God anointed Jesus of Nazareth with the Holy Ghost and with power: who went about doing good, and healing all that were oppressed of the devil; for God was with him. And we are witnesses of all things which He did both in the land of the Jews, and in Jerusalem; whom they slew and hanged on a tree: Him God raised up the third day, and shewed him openly; Not to all the people, but unto witnesses chosen before of God, even to us, who did eat and drink with Him after He rose from the dead. And He commanded us to preach unto the people, and to testify that it is He which was ordained of God to be the Judge of quick and dead. To Him give all the prophets witness, that through His name whosoever believeth in Him shall receive remission of sins.[37]

---

[37] Acts 10:38 KJV.

CHAPTER 3

REDEMPTION

Redemption is all through the Old Testament and part of a firm foundation because it is about God the Father restoring man back into the proper fellowship. Mankind was in need of a redeemer after the fall of Adam in the garden. He willfully disobeyed God and ate from the tree of good and evil. The sin of Adam was the crime of high treason. Christ later paid the penalty so that man could be given eternal life and stand before God as though he had never sinned. Therefore, God had a plan to redeem man back to Himself. *Redeem* is defined as to buy back, rescue, or ransom for.

Three purposes are distinguishable in each of the Old Testament books: the historical, the doctrinal, and the Christological. Respectively, these purposes include what the book aimed to accomplished in the lives of the original listeners for whom it was written and what the book tells us about Christ the coming Messiah.

The thread of redemption is woven from Genesis to Revelation. The Old Testament shows us the types and shadows of the coming Redeemer. In the book of Ruth, we see a good example of a redeemer. The book of Ruth beautifully portrays several messianic purposes. It shows how Christ, our Kinsman Redeemer, purchases us for Himself. One very significant doctrinal emphasis of the book of Ruth is its demonstration of the function of the view concerning the Kinsman Redeemer.

There are Messianic prophecies of the Redeemer. Isaiah 61:1 says, "The Spirit of the Lord God is upon Me, because the LORD has anointed Me to preach good tidings to the poor; He has sent Me to heal the brokenhearted, to proclaim liberty to the captives, and the opening of the prison to those who are bound."

In the beginning of man's fellowship with God, there were no walls of separation. Adam walked with God in the garden of Eden in the cool of the day.

Adam broke that fellowship by disobeying God. God had devised a plan called redemption that would restore man back to His rightful position with God. Genesis 1:1 says, "In the beginning God created the heavens and the earth."[38]

The word *God* in the Hebrew is "Elohim." This word is plural, revealing the Trinity at work in creation. John 1:1–3 and Colossians 1:16 reveal that Christ had a major part in the great acts of creation.[39] Psalm 104:30 and Genesis 1:2 show the Holy Spirit's work in creation.[40] You see, He was in the beginning a Father God. In eternity, He had a Father nature. We can understand a father's love and desire for children. Our civilization is built around this fact, for the home is the basic unit of society.

Before God created a world, in His plan, man was marked out for sonship. He was to be the answer to the Father's hunger for children. When a man

---

[38] Genesis 1:1 KJV.

[39] John 1:1–3 KJV, Colossians 1:16. KJV

[40] Psalm 104:30 KJV, Genesis 1:2. KJV

is born again and really experiences Jesus, he will see the character of God. Because man can form a mental picture of Christ, he has developed the habit of praying to Christ, praising, and worshipping Him alone. The renewing of the man's mind by the Word of God brings an awareness of the Father to him that revolutionizes his life.

When man was created, he was planned as a perfect human being with an endless human life. Adam's body was perfect and fit to be the temple of God's underruler. He was the object of God's love and affection. It was the joy of the Father to give His man dominion over the works He had created. This man had, by creation, the ability to rule the universe.[41]

God had conferred upon him the authority to rule the universe. This universe-wide dominion was the most sacred heritage God could give to man. Adam turned this legal dominion over into the hands of God's enemy, Satan. Adam's transgression was done in absolute knowledge. He was not deceived by Satan.

---

[41] Genesis 1:28 KJV, Psalm 8:6.

He understood the steps that led to the crime of high treason.

We have come to one of the most interesting features of Redemption in the Bible. Adam had legally conferred to Satan the authority with which God had vested him. God's grace made provision for humanity's redemption. Note this authority was not given to Satan by God. God the Father would never confer to His enemy dominion over His creation and man, the object of His love. This was all Adam's doing when he obeyed the voice of Satan instead of the voice of God the Father. Satan tempted man in the garden because of his bitter hatred toward God. He knew what man meant to the Father God. It became his object to separate this union and bring humanity under bondage to himself and destruction. He knew this would cause God the greatest suffering. Yet, Satan, in his malignant character, could not foresee that God would suffer by His own will for this man until He brought him back to Himself. God's triumph over Satan at Calvary reveals the Father's love for His children. He was not willing to lose them to Satan.

The first prophecy of redemption, the coming of the Redeemer, is this: "And I will put enmity between thee and the woman, between thy seed and her Seed, He shall bruise thy head, and thou shalt bruise His heel." This is saying that Jesus will be born to restore mankind back into proper fellowship with God the father. Here is a prophecy that a woman shall give birth to a child independent of natural conception[42]

God makes the promise of the Redeemer more specific. A family is marked "the seed of Abraham"[43] and "seed of David."[44] God makes it more specific when He says, "Behold the Virgin shall conceive and bear a son, and call His Name Immanuel."[45]

God is preserving a line through which the Redeemer shall come, a righteous line. The third son born to Adam and Eve was Seth. It was he through whom the righteous line would come. In this line

---

[42] Genesis 3:15 KJV.

[43] Genesis 12:3 KJV.

[44] Psalm 89:3–4 KJV.

[45] Isaiah 7:14 KJV.

came Noah, Shem, Abraham, Jacob, and then later on, Jesus Himself. The Sethites walked with God. The seventh in the line of Seth was Enoch, a man who had this testimony, that he pleased God. We see again the working of Satan to thwart the purpose of God. He causes the intermarriage of the line of Cain with the righteous line. This corrupts the line through which the Redeemer shall come to such an extent that only Noah is left.

Three hundred and sixty-seven years after the flood, Abraham appeared. Noah was alive for fifty years after the birth of Abraham.[46] Abraham lived among ungodly people for seventy-five years. He was born and lived in Ur of the Chaldees until he received his call from God. At this time, the revelation of God was little.

God had to choose one man who knew Him and make a nation that would preserve the knowledge of Himself upon the earth. Twenty-five years after Abraham had received his call from God, the greatest

---

[46] Isaiah 41:8 KJV.

event in human history until the birth of Christ took place. It was the blood covenant into which Jehovah and Abraham had entered. God came to Abraham to make a covenant with him. This blood covenant was called the Covenant of Strong Friendship. That is why Abraham was called the friend of God.[47] We must gather the firm foundation of redemption because God swore by no greater; He swore by Himself.

---

[47] 2 Chronicles 20:7 KJV.

CHAPTER 4

SALVATION

It is an important part of a firm foundation that you understand what salvation is so that you may receive it as a gift and benefit from its blessings. The Bible talks about it in Romans 3:21–5:21.

What is salvation? Salvation is deliverance and freedom from the authority and control of sin. According to the Word of God, you will be saved from enemies (Luke 1:71), sin (Romans 10:1, 9–10), bondage (Acts 7:25), sickness, and disease (Acts 4:12).

Salvation comes from the Greek word *soteria*, which means deliverance. Salvation, in the New Testament, refers to eternal and temporary deliverance from danger. Deliverance is a release from bondage, imprisonment, and captivity. Moreover, salvation is a gift available to all who repent and change their attitude to and direction away from sin. One must believe in Jesus, which prepares you to confess Him as your Lord and Savior.

What does salvation cost me? The price of salvation was paid by the blood of Jesus Christ. Jesus paid the price for you to receive the gift of salvation. What does knowing Jesus have to do with my salvation? Jesus is the only way to the Father, according to John 14:6.

We have to be careful in using the word *salvation* because it has been confused in some religious circles with the term *born again*, even though these two terms are not synonymous. They are related ideas, but they do not mean exactly the same thing. The word *salvation* is used in the Bible to indicate a work of God on behalf of man. So salvation is the result of the work of God for the individual rather than the work of the individual for God.

Becoming born again is what happens to your spirit after you repent, confess with your mouth the Lord Jesus Christ, and believe in your heart that God raised Him from the dead. To be born again means to move from darkness into light. So, being born again involves a transition, or translation, from one point to another point, from one position to another position, based on a decision that you make.

However, salvation is what is available to you when you become born again, and it is not just something that's stored up in heaven for you in the sweet by-and-by. It's not something you have to leave the earth in the Rapture in order to receive. Salvation is what you have available to you right here and now as a born-again person. The word *salvation* in the New Testament means healing, safety, deliverance, protection, and soundness and including the ministry of angels.

Therefore, God is saying that angels have been sent to serve the heirs ofsalvation.. They have the responsibility of serving you if you're a born-again person. The angels are to serve you in the areas of healing, deliverance, safety, protection, and soundness, and they are to minister to you in any other area where you have need.

The heart of God's plan of salvation is focused on the purpose and function of a Mediator, One who could go between God and a helpless, sinful man. "We must see that the righteousness of God is by faith in Jesus Christ not by the law."[48]

Jesus has opened the door of salvation to every person, and I have received Jesus for myself. Thank God, Jesus has opened the door of salvation that no one can shut—unless the person him- or herself refuses to walk through that open door by not receiving Jesus Christ as his or her Savior.

What does it mean that Jesus is the Door to salvation? Remember, Jesus said, "I am the door, by me if any man enter in, he shall be saved ..."[49] Then in Hebrews 10:20, the Bible says, "By a new and living way, which He (Jesus) hath consecrated for us, through the veil, that is to say, His flesh." Paul talks about it too: "God hath quickened us together

---

[48] Romans 3:21.

[49] John 10:9 KJV.

with Christ."[50] In other words, by shedding His blood on the Cross at Calvary, Jesus opened the door of salvation to every person who would ever live on this earth. Paul explains in Galatians 3 that when Jesus died and shed His blood for the remission of our sins, the curtain that separated the Holy of Holies from the Holy place was split in two. That partition separated man from the Holy of Holies, where the presence of God dwelt under the Old Covenant.[51] Once that partition was rent by the sacrifice of Jesus's own body on the cross of Calvary, the presence of God was no longer contained in a man-made tabernacle.[52] By the sacrifice of Jesus, the presence of God came to dwell in every person who would receive Jesus Christ as his or her Savior.[53] Jesus Himself is the Door of salvation because He made the way for all people to be saved by sacrificing Himself. And Jesus called Himself the

---

[50] Ephesians 2:5–6.

[51] Romans 3:25.

[52] Colossians 1:27.

[53] John 14:23 KJV.

Door. In fact, there is no other door through which we can receive salvation or eternal life (Acts 4:12).

The Resurrection of Christ is absolutely central to establish the salvation of the Christian religion. There would have been no Christianity if the belief in the resurrection had not been established in *soteriology.* The essential teaching of Christianity is the belief of the resurrection. *Soteriology* is the study of the work of God on behalf of man. This clearly states that if Christ be not raised, then our faith is also vain.

Who else in all human history but Jesus Christ ever said he would come back from the dead after His death. It is a fact that Jesus publicly announced He would rise from the dead. He also predicted He would do so on the third day. No one ever has made that claim. Before the triumphal entry into Jerusalem, Jesus said that the chief priests and scribes would condemn Him to death. Because Jesus did what he said, we can today know that salvation is real.

In the Old Covenant, God had manifested Himself to Israel as one God. This was a startling revelation to man at a time when he was surrounded by a sea of polytheism. Then, after many centuries, when God came to earth in the person of His Son, He was presented as Three in One. In the Old Testament, the Holy Spirit only came on man not into them.

As we know the life of Christ, we are conscious of the Three Who Are One. At the beginning of His public life, at His baptism, the voice of the Father spoke out of heaven, saying, "this is my beloved Son," and the Spirit descended visibly upon Him in the form of a dove.[54] Here a threefold revelation of God is given to man on the level of his physical senses. In Christ's teaching, preaching, and private conversation, He constantly spoke of His Father and Himself as two distinct persons and yet declared equality: "I and My Father are One." Again, He said, "He who has seen Me hath seen the Father."[55]

In His teachings, a third is brought in as being God also. In His last and longest recorded talk with

---

[54] Matthew 3:16–17 KJV.
[55] John 10:30 KJV.

His disciples, which occurred in the upper room the evening before His crucifixion, Christ said, "The Holy Spirit, whom the Father will send in My name, He shall teach you all things and bring to your remembrance all that I said unto you."[56] A major part of Christ's last talk with the disciples dealt with the Holy Spirit, who was to come to take His place. This message is recorded in the fourteenth and sixteenth chapters of the Gospel of John. Everything in the description in the Bible of the Three called Father, Son, and Holy Spirit presents definitely and absolutely no more and no less than three Persons in the Godhead.

When Jesus was about to leave the disciples, He promised that He would send the Holy Spirit into the world to become their Teacher, Guide, and Comforter. The Holy Spirit was going to have charge of the ministry and the work of the church. He was to overshadow the church, and they were to walk in His presence.

---

[56] John 14:26 KJV.

He was to come also into the individual member's body to take up His abode there so that He might govern the person's actions, think through his or her mind, love through his or her affections, and will through his or her will; the believer's body was to be His permanent home. I want you to notice that the Holy Spirit is a person. In Matthew 28:19, Jesus says, "Go ye into all the world and make disciples of all the nations, baptizing them in the name of the Father, and of the Son, and of the Holy Spirit."

Christ as a man could be seen and touched by man; therefore, His ministry has been more real to us than the ministry and Person of the Holy Spirit, who cannot be contacted through the physical senses. We may form a mental picture of Christ but not of the Holy Spirit.

The purpose of the Holy Spirit's ministry upon the earth is not the same as that of Christ's earthly ministry. Christ came to pay, as man's substitute, the penalty of Adam's high treason. That demanded that He identify Himself with man. Therefore, He has been revealed to us as a man, in a body like ours. Christ's earthly ministry was also local. He could be in only one place on earth at one time. Now He has His position as Mediator between God and man.

The Holy Spirit could not come in a human body as Christ came. His ministry could not be fulfilled in that manner. His ministry could not be localized. He came to impart the nature of God to the spirit of man.

He came not in a human body but to indwell the bodies of those who had become new creations in Christ. Yet His coming was as positive and as definitive as the coming of Christ in the Incarnation.

Paul believed that as we truly understand salvation or *soteria*, we can walk in the fullness of what Jesus has obtained for us. Because of what Jesus has done, we can walk in true deliverance. Sin can no longer hold us in bondage or the Law.

Remember, salvation comes from the Greek word *soteria*, which means deliverance, healing, health, safety, soundness, and wholeness. Deliverance is a release from bondage, imprisonment, and captivity.

Paul also believed the free gift of salvation is available to all who repent and believe in Jesus. Whosoever confesses Jesus as Savior and Lord can be saved. Jesus died for your sins so that you can have the abundant life of prosperity and health!

Jesus paid the price by shedding His own blood for your salvation. Shedding His blood on Calvary, Jesus opened the door of salvation to whosoever would believe on Him. Jesus paid the price for you to receive the gift of salvation.

Jesus is the only way to the Father, and there is no other name under heaven by which we may be saved. So the name gets us born-again, and the name also keeps us safe. Salvation is an important part of a firm foundation so that you may receive the gift and benefit from its blessings in every arena of life.

CHAPTER 5

COVENANT-MINDED GOD

God is a covenant-minded God, and His covenant gives us access to His promises, securing our firm foundation. In His infinite understanding of our human weakness and need, God knows there is no possible way in which men can pledge their faithfulness. God gives us perfect confidence in His covenant and the full assurance of all that He is and His infinite riches, power, and promises for us.

Blessed is the man who truly knows God as his Covenant God, who knows what the Covenant promises to him. This unwavering confidence of expectation secures all that will be fulfilled by God. The claim of the covenant, which God Himself keeps with man, is bestowed upon us. This means having the full knowledge of what God wants to do for us and the assurance that it will be done by God Almighty and being drawn to Him in personal surrender.

In every covenant, there are usually two parties. A covenant is defined as a binding and solid agreement, made by two or more individuals to do or keep from doing a specific thing.[57] Every foundation of a covenant is based on each party being faithful to the part it has undertaken to perform. Unfaithfulness on either side breaks the covenant. As an end of enmity or uncertainty, as a statement of services and benefits to be rendered, as a security for their certain performance, as a bond of amity and goodwill, as a ground for perfect confidence and friendship, a covenant has often been of unspeakable value.

When God created man in His image and likeness, it was that he might have a life as like His own as it was possible for a creature to live. The secret of man's happiness is to trustfully surrender his whole being to the will of God. When sin entered, the relationship

---

[57] *Webster's Dictionary* (The World Publishing Company, 1960), 339.

with God was broken. When man disobeyed, he feared God and fled from Him.

"Know therefore that the Lord thy God, He is God, the faithful God, which keepeth covenant and mercy with them that love Him and keep His commandments."[58]

Don't run from God; run *to* God. All God wants man to do is to believe in Him. Salvation is only by faith, and God restores the life man had lost. A man in faith who yields himself to God will have safety. In entering into covenant with us, God's objective is to draw us to Him in order to render us entirely dependent upon Him. "They shall be My people, and I will be their God. And I will make an everlasting covenant with them, that I will not turn away from them to do them good …"[59]

God will not break His covenant. In the Old Covenant, God said to Israel, "Obey My voice, and

---

58 Deuteronomy 7:9 KJV.
59 Jeremiah 32:38 KJV.

I will be your God."[60] These simple words contained the whole covenant. The question of Israel having the ability to obey was not taken into consideration; disobedience caused them to forfeit the privileges of the covenant. God as Creator could never take His people into His favor and fellowship, except if they obeyed Him. The New Covenant is better than the Old, because it is an everlasting Covenant, never to be broken.

This is the glory of the New Covenant, the glory that has excelled and the glory that has His provision made. The glory is a supernatural mystery of divine wisdom and grace, that no human mind could ever devise.

It is just because of this, that man cannot take credit or mess it up. The essential part of the New Covenant that exceeds and confounds all our thoughts of what a covenant means. Man has not been able to see his inheritance. People have not been able to see and believe what the New Covenant really means.

---

[60] Jeremiah 7:23, 11:4 KJV.

The New Covenant gives us eternal love from God and His ways rather than only an obedience with His Word. We have thought that human unfaithfulness was the only factor permanently to be reckoned with as something utterly unconquerable and incurable. Man has therefore sought to stir the mind to its utmost by arguments and motives and never realized how the Holy Spirit is to be the unceasing, all-sufficient worker of everything that has to be wrought by the Christian.

Listen to God's word in Ezekiel, in regard to one of the terms of His covenant of peace, His everlasting covenant. "I will put my Spirit within you, and cause you to walk in my statutes, and ye shall keep My judgments, and do them."[61] In the Old Covenant, we have nothing of this kind. On the contrary, from the story of the golden calf and the breaking of the Tablets of the Covenant onward, the sad fact is continual departure from God.

---

[61] Ezekiel 36:27 KJV.

We find throughout the book of Deuteronomy, without parallel, in the history of any religion or religious lawgiver, that Moses most distinctly prophesies their forsaking of God, with the terrible curses and dispersion that would come upon them.

The supreme difference of the New Covenant— the one thing for which the Mediator, the Blood, and the Spirit were given; the one fruit God sought and Himself engaged to bring forth—was the following characteristic: a heart filled with His fear and love, a heart to cleave unto Him and not depart from him, a heart in which His Spirit and His law dwells, and a heart that delights to do His will.

The secret of the New Covenant deals with the heart of man in divine power. It not only appeals to the heart by every motive of fear and love but by duty and gratitude. The New Covenant reveals God Himself cleansing our heart and making it new, changing it entirely from a stony heart into a heart of flesh, a tender, living, loving heart. He put His Spirit within it, and so, by His almighty power and love, breathing and working in it, making the promise true, "I will cause you to walk in My statutes ..." created a heart in perfect harmony with Him. God has engaged in a covenant to work this in us. He undertakes for our part in the covenant as much as for His own.

This is the restoration of the original relation between God and man, whom He had made in His likeness. He was on earth to be the very image of God, because God was to live and to work all in him to find his glory. This is the exceeding glory of the New Covenant. Pentecost changed the rules. The Holy Spirit could now again be the indwelling life of His people and so make the promise a reality.

My brother or sister, the great sin of Israel under the Old Covenant, which greatly grieved Him, was that they limited the Holy One of Israel. Under the New Covenant, there is no less danger of this sin. It makes it impossible for God to fulfill His promises. Let us seek for the teaching of the Holy Spirit, to show us exactly what God has established the New Covenant for, that we may honor Him by believing all that His love has prepared for us. Although God has provided all of this, we must make that decision to appropriate it into our life.

The blood is one of the strongest, deepest, mightiest, and most heavenly of the thoughts of God. It lies at the very root of both covenants but especially of the New Covenant. The difference between the two covenants is the difference between the blood of beasts and the blood of the Lamb of God! The power of the new Covenant has no lesser measure than the worth of the blood of the Son of God! Your Christian experience ought to know of the standard of peace with God, purity from sin, and power over the world that the blood of Christ can give. If we would enter truly and fully into all the New Covenant is meant to be to us, let us go to God to reveal to us the worth and the power of the blood of the covenant, the precious blood of Christ!

The first Covenant was brought in by blood. There could be no Covenant of friendship between a holy God and sinful men without atonement and reconciliation and no atonement without a death as the penalty of sin. God said, "I have given you the blood upon the altar to make atonement for your souls; for it is the blood that maketh atonement for the soul." The blood shed in death meant the death of a sacrifice slain for the sin of man; the blood sprinkled on the altar meant that vicarious death was accepted of God for the sinful one. No forgiveness, no covenant without bloodshedding.

All this was but type and shadow of what was one day to become a mysterious reality. No thought of man or angel could have conceived what even now passes all understanding: the Eternal Son of God took flesh and blood and then shed that blood as the blood of the New Covenant not merely to ratify it but to open the way for it and to make it possible. "Behold the Blood of the covenant, which the Lord hath made with you."[62]

Until we learn to form our expectation of a life in the New Covenant, according to the inconceivable

---

[62] Hebrews 9:20 KJV.

worth and power of the blood of God's Son, we never can have even an insight into the entire supernatural and heavenly life that a child of God may live.

In the passage from Hebrews 9:15, we read, "For this cause Christ is the Mediator of a new covenant, that a death having taken place for the redemption of the transgressions that were under the first covenant ..." The sins of the ages, of the First Covenant, which had only figuratively been atoned for, had gathered up before God. A death was needed for the redemption of these: In that death and bloodshedding of the Lamb of God, not only were these atoned for but the power of all sin was forever broken.

The blood of the New Covenant is redemption blood, a purchase price and ransom from the power of sin and the Law. In any purchase made on earth, the transference of property from the old owner to the new is complete. Its worth may be ever so great and the hold on it ever so strong, but if the price be paid, it is gone forever from him who owned it. The hold sin had on us was terrible. No thought can realize its legitimate claim on us under God's law, its awful tyrannical power enslaving us. But the blood of God's Son has paid. "Ye were redeemed, not with corruptible things as silver and gold ..." We have been rescued, ransomed, redeemed out of our old natural life under the power of sin, utterly and eternally. Sin has not the slightest claim on us, nor the slightest power over us, except as our ignorance or unbelief or half-heartedness allows it to have dominion. Our New Covenant birthright is to stand in the freedom with which Christ has made us free. Until the spirit man sees, desires, accepts, and claims the redemption and the liberty that has the blood of the Son of God for its purchase price, its measure, and its security, it can never fully live the New Covenant life.

On account of sin, there could be no covenant between man and God without the blood of the Son of God. As the cleansing away of sins was the first condition in making a covenant, so it is equally the first condition of an entrance into it. It has ever been found that a deeper appropriation of the blessings of the Covenant must be preceded by a new and deeper cleaning from sin.

God said, "I will make a Covenant of peace with them; it shall be an everlasting Covenant with them." So walk in your covenant rights that Jesus made for you.

God has covenant on His mind when He thinks of you and me. He has made provision for the total covenant to be on Him. Because He knows man's weaknesses and short-comings, God binds Himself by covenant so that man can have confidence and faith in Him, that man can have full assurance that God is a covenant-keeping God.

As we lay hold to the covenant of God, we will see the Almighty bring His Word to pass, but we have to surrender all to the Lord. We must not forget that it is His faithfulness that secures everything. This is not based on what man can do but what God has done and will do concerning His covenant.

Part of this covenant is man's heart. It will be changed from a stony heart, and he will be given a heart of flesh. By this, God can do a work in the life of His covenant people. This covenant is an everlasting covenant. This covenant will bring peace. This covenant came with the price of blood. "This cup is the new covenant in My blood."[63] "The blood of the covenant, wherewith He was sanctified."[64] You are in covenant with God Himself! God is a covenant-minded God, and His covenant gives us access to His promises, securing our firm foundation as a believer.

---

[63] 1 Corinthians 11:25 KJV.

[64] Hebrews 10:29 KJV.

CHAPTER 6

THE HOLY SPIRIT

The Holy Spirit–empowered church is first. God can empower us to resist the temptations of the devil best by the Holy Spirit living in our bodies. The Holy Spirit is the guarantee for our firm foundation. This scripture then becomes true: "Greater is He that is in you than he that is in the world."[65]

He may be our Teacher, Guide, and Comforter. He may empower us for testimony and service. He may make the Father and Jesus real to our spirits. One reason for the weakness of the church today is that it believes the Holy Spirit was simply with man and not in man. The guarantee we have today in our firm foundation is that He constantly resides in us.

Importantly, we know that we are God's children; we are living in fellowship with Him. We also

---

[65] 1 John 4:4 KJV

recognize the Lordship of Jesus over our lives, and we know that we have a legal right to His indwelling. In simple confidence, we can go to the Father and ask Him in Jesus's name to give us the Holy Spirit, and He will, just as He gave us eternal life when we took Christ as our Savior, for His Word cannot be broken. "How much more shall your heavenly Father give the Holy Spirit to them that ask Him." [66]

After many centuries, when God came to earth in the person of His Son, He was presented as Three in One. No one can claim to be a believer if they don't believe in the tri-unity of the Godhead.

As we know the life of Christ, we are conscious of the Three Who Are One. At the beginning of His public life, at His baptism, the voice of the Father spoke out of heaven, "This is my beloved Son," and the Spirit descended visibly upon Him in the form of a dove.[67] Here, a threefold revelation of God is given to man on the level of his physical senses.

---

[66] Luke 11:13 KJV

[67] Matthew 3:16–17 KJV.

In Christ's teaching, preaching, and private conversation, He constantly spoke of His Father and Himself as two distinct persons and yet equal. "I and My Father are One." Again He said, "He who has seen Me hath seen the Father."[68]

In His teachings, a Third is brought in as being God also. In His last and longest recorded talk with His disciples in the upper room the evening before His crucifixion, Christ said, "The Holy Spirit, whom the Father will send in My name, He shall teach you all things and bring to your remembrance all that I said unto you."[69] A major part of Christ's last talk with the disciples dealt with the Holy Spirit, who was to come to take His place. This message is recorded in the fourteenth and sixteenth chapters of the Gospel of John. Everything in the Bible's description of the Three called Father, Son, and Holy Spirit presents definitely and absolutely no more and no less than Three Persons in the Godhead.

---

[68] John 10:30 KJV.
[69] John 14:26 KJV.

David A. Burgess

When Jesus was about to leave the disciples, He promised that He would send the Holy Spirit into the world to become their Teacher, Guide, and Comforter. The Holy Spirit was going to have charge of the ministry and the work of the church. He was to overshadow the church, and they were to walk in His presence.

He was to come also into the individual member's body to take up His abode there so that He might govern his or her actions, think through his or her mind, and love through his or her affections. The body was to be His permanent home. The Holy Spirit is a person. In Matthew 28:19, Jesus says, "Go ye into all the world and make disciples of all the nations, baptizing them in the name of the Father, and of the Son, and of the Holy Spirit." Here, Jesus gives the Holy Spirit the same place, the same personality, and the same honor that He gives to the Father and to Himself.

Christ as a man could be seen and touched by man; therefore, His ministry has been more real to us than the ministry and person of the Holy Spirit, who cannot be contacted through the physical senses. We may form a mental picture of Christ, while we cannot of the Holy Spirit.

The purpose of the Holy Spirit's ministry upon the earth is not the same as that of Christ's earthly ministry. Christ came to pay, as man's substitute, the penalty of Adam's high treason. The demand of Jesus was by man's sin. Therefore, He has been revealed to us as a man, in a body like ours. Christ's earthly ministry was local. He could be in only one place on earth at one time. Now He has His position as Mediator between God and man.

The Holy Spirit could not come in a human body as Christ came. His ministry could not be fulfilled in that manner. His ministry could not be localized. He came to impart the nature of God to the spirit of man.

Yet His coming was as positive, as definite as the coming of Christ in the Incarnation. He is the third person of the Godhead. He is actually here upon earth, working in and through the body of Christ.

The coming of the Holy Spirit was foretold by Jesus. Christ's coming to earth was foretold by prophets and angels. Christ Himself foretold the advent of the Holy Spirit into the world in His last discourses with His disciples. He foretold the coming of the One who was equal with Himself and who should take His place.

Read John 14:16–20, 15:26–27, 16:1–16 and Acts 1:4–5. The Holy Spirit did not come on this divine mission until the Day of Pentecost. He had been the divine agent in creation. In the creation of the physical world, He had imparted life, form, and the power of development to dead and formless matter.

The Holy Spirit could not come until Christ had been glorified. Christ had to die for man's offenses, rise when man had been declared righteous (Romans 4:25), and enter into the Holy of Holies with His own blood, obtaining eternal redemption for man (Hebrews 9:12).

Let us now study carefully all that scripture teaches about being baptized with the Holy Spirit. It is first mentioned by John: "He shall baptize you with the Holy Spirit and fire."[70]

After His Resurrection, Christ refers to this promise made by John, "Commanding them not to depart from Jerusalem but to wait for the promise from the Father" (Acts 1:5). The term *baptize* is also used in Acts 11:16 by Peter when he is speaking of the fact that the Holy Spirit came upon the Gentiles in exactly the same manner as He did upon the Jews on the Day of Pentecost.

The word *baptize* is an untranslated Greek word meaning to "immerse." John had merely immersed them in water, but there was soon to come an immersion in the Holy Spirit.

Then Paul speaks of the baptism with the Holy Spirit in 1 Corinthians 12:13: "For by one Spirit are we all baptized into one body."

Galatians 3:27 says, "For as many of you as have been baptized into Christ have put on Christ."

---

[70] Matthew 3:11 KJV

On the Day of Pentecost, the Holy Spirit entered the world for His special ministry. It was as definite a coming as the birth of Christ as a babe in Bethlehem. He filled the room where they were sitting. The miraculous happened. The room was filled with the Holy Spirit, and they were immersed, or baptized, with the Holy Spirit.

There are several phrases used in reference to Pentecost: "coming upon," "pour out," "fallen upon," "fell upon," "poured forth," "fell on them," "came upon." The result was immersion in the Holy Spirit, out of which came the New Birth.

The body of Christ was born on that memorable day. As the manger had been the cradle of the Son of God, so also the upper room became the cradle of the body of Christ.

But even after you become a new creation, God's desire and plan is that you receive the baptism in the Holy Spirit. Your baptism in the Holy Spirit is received by faith. Jesus said in Luke 11:13, "... how much more shall your heavenly Father give the Holy Spirit to them that ask Him?"

When you ask in faith, the Holy Spirit comes to live in you. And when you are filled with the Holy Spirit, as the believers were in the book of Acts, you speak in tongues. Speaking in tongues simply is speaking in a language that only God understands—even you won't understand it. This happens as the Holy Spirit prays through you about things you may not know about or may not know how to pray about (Romans 8:6).

The Holy Spirit was sent to be our helper. So when you pray in tongues, what actually happens is that the Holy Spirit searches your heart and prays through you the perfect will of God.[71] You actually utter secret truths and hidden things that are not obvious to the understanding of your mind.[72]

To pray in tongues, you need to realize that the unknown tongue is the language of your heart. Known

---

[71] Romans 8:26 KJV.

[72] 1 Corinthians 14:2 KJV.

tongues are the languages of the human mind (unless one of the vocal gifts of the nine gift of the Spirit is in operation).

The Holy Spirit of God will give you utterance, the same as your mind gives you thought to speak. To speak in tongues, you must cooperate with the Holy Spirit. The Apostle Paul said in 1 Corinthians 14:14, "For if I pray in an [unknown] tongue, my spirit [by the Holy Spirit within me] prays, but my mind is unproductive …"

Notice that was Paul who did the speaking. Ask the Holy Spirit to take charge of your tongue, and then yield your tongue to His use. You cannot speak in your own language and tongues at the same time, just as you cannot speak in English and French at the same time.

When your voice and tongue begin forming syllables around the expression that your heart desires to release, you will also speak in tongues. It will be your tongue, your breath, and your vocal cords, and you will be actively forming words. You will supply the sounds, but the Holy Spirit will supply the words—words unknown to you. It may seem awkward to you at first, but continue. Like a child learning to speak, you will grow.

Finally, as you seek the baptism in the Holy Spirit, you need not wait to get a word from God about it; you already have His Word. Nor do you need to wait around for the Spirit. The Spirit of God entered His ministry on the Day of Pentecost, and He has been here ever since. He has never left!

Furthermore, you need not be concerned over being deceived by the devil and ending up with something that is from him. When you ask your heavenly Father for one of His promises—in this case, the baptism in the Holy Spirit—you can be confident that the gift given is from God, not Satan. "The invisible persuader concerning Christ is within you."[73]

---

[73] Mike Murdock, *The Holy Spirit* (The Wisdom Center, 1997), 30.

One of the most stirring books of the Bible is the book of Acts. It has always thrilled me to read it and see how mightily God worked through the church in those days. But for years, one thing about it has bothered me. I couldn't understand why the church in Acts was so much more powerful than the church today.

In this present day, many people have never even heard the message of the Christ. Despite the fact that a large percentage of present-day believers frequently use the word *Christ* to refer to the Lord Jesus, despite the fact that we've used Christ to identify entire denominations, very few people even know what the word means, much less understand the message behind it. That's because Christ is not an English word. It's a Greek word.

Translators have neglected to translate the Greek for so many years. Because of the lack of translation research, generations of Christians have missed out on major scriptural revelation. For hundreds of years, Western believers have ignorantly used the word *Christ* as if it were Jesus's last name or even a religious title. The truth is the word *Christ* means "anointed."

Although we generally think of the word *anointed* in a spiritual context, the word in and of itself isn't spiritual. *Anointed* simply means "poured over."

But when you begin to talk about Jesus being the Christ, the One who has been sent by God and anointed with God's delivering power, the word becomes very, very special.

If you're a Christian, then you're anointed because the very word *Christian* is derived from the Greek word *Christ*, which, as mentioned, means "the Anointed One." Translate the word *Christian*, and you'll find out it means to be anointed like Him!

In fact, to say you're anything less than anointed is to reject the inheritance Jesus purchased for you with His own precious blood. Jesus didn't go to the cross and pay the price for sin just so you could be average. He did it so you could be cleansed and become a temple of the Holy Spirit, who is the anointing (2 Corinthians 6:16).

Jesus suffered, died, and rose again so that He could give birth to a new race of reborn men and women who would be equipped with His own anointing. Jesus laid down His life so that He could raise up a race of believers who would walk this earth, doing not only the same works that He Himself did but even greater works![74]

The very thought of doing the works of Jesus staggers the minds of most Christians today. They just can't see how such a thing could be possible. No doubt, the first disciples felt the same way. Especially after the Crucifixion when they scattered and ran in fear, they must have wondered what Jesus could possibly have meant when He'd said to them, "It's expedient for you that I go away."

Then everything changed. Jesus rose from the dead. He met with the disciples and instructed them

---

[74] John 14:12 KJV.

to remain in Jerusalem and wait for the promise of the Father. The disciples were thinking about the fact that Christ, the One anointed with God's own mighty Spirit and power, had just told them He was going to immerse them in that same power! They were thinking about the message Jesus started preaching after He was baptized with the Holy Spirit in the Jordan River. They'd heard it many times: "The Spirit of the Lord is upon Me."

Peter, in particular, was probably thinking of the revelation he had blurted out one day when Jesus had asked, "Whom say ye that I am?" Peter, perhaps better than anyone, knew what the anointing could do. He saw how the anointing operated in Jesus's life. As a fisherman, he'd seen Jesus draw every fish in the river of Galilee around his boat.

There were no theologians there to calm him down and tell him God's miracle-working power had passed away. All Peter knew was "Jesus is the Anointed of God, the Son of the living God, and now His Anointing has come on us!"

Why aren't believers today as excited about the baptism of the Holy Spirit as Peter was? Why, instead of charging out into the world and turning it upside down with the power of God like those first disciples did, do most modern-day believers do little more with the anointing than talk in tongues now and then?

For the most part, it's because we have had such a limited revelation of what can actually happen when the anointing of Jesus operates through us.

Even Christians who have some understanding of the anointing often think of it only in terms of the ministry. They think it operates primarily through apostles, prophets, pastors, teachers, and evangelists, usually within the context of a church service or meeting. But the fact is, there is an anointing through Jesus by the Holy Ghost, whom the Father has sent in His name, to do any and every righteous act on the face of this earth, through any person who knows Him as Lord. In other words, no matter what God has called you to do, there is an anointing available to help you carry that out.

We've been mistaken to think that only preachers are anointed. All believers are anointed. If you know Jesus and you're baptized in His Spirit, you can expect the spiritual gifts or manifestations of the Spirit to work in your life as you need them.[75]

These gifts are available to anyone who knows God. Of course, we don't choose our own gifts and how they operate. The Holy Spirit causes them to function as He wills and for the service of His kingdom. You may experience one particular manifestation of the Holy Ghost because you're in a situation where it's necessary and then never again experience that particular manifestation.

Although you may not know exactly how the anointing will manifest, you can have faith it will manifest in some way because you've been called to be a witness. The Holy Spirit intends to use you wherever you are as a witness to the fact that Jesus of Nazareth is anointed with the Holy Ghost and power. He intends to use you to demonstrate the fact

---

[75] 1 Corinthians 12:7 KJV.

that Jesus is still going about doing good, healing those who are oppressed of the devil, and He is doing it through you!

The apostle John already said it! In 1 John 2:27, he wrote, "But the anointing which ye have received of Him (Jesus) abideth in you ..." The word *abide* means to remain "continually." So that scripture is telling us that if we'll remain continually in Jesus, His anointing will remain continually available to us.

We haven't even scratched the surface of that glorious truth yet! We haven't even begun to see what can happen in our lives if we'll just learn to receive the anointing by faith, stop hindering it, and let it flow. When we step fully into the anointing Jesus has made available to us, we won't just sit around saying, "Praise the Lord," and feeling spiritual goose bumps. We'll start seeing the real, supernatural, *dunamis* power of God at work.

So get out your Bible, and start studying. Every time you see the word *Christ*, translate it and meditate on the fact that it means "the anointed one" and "His anointing." Learn how to protect the anointing and how to live your life in such a way that the Holy Ghost can work freely through you. The Holy Spirit is the guarantee of our covenant and firm foundation.

CONCLUSION

We have discussed that which I believe will set you on course for a firm foundation of your Christian journey. A firm foundation is a blueprint for a pattern of success in our Christian lives. With diligence in studying faith, Jesus, redemption, salvation, covenant, and the Holy Spirit, you will secure a firm foundation in a victorious Christian life. The Holy Spirit is the guarantee of our covenant and firm foundation. His covenant gives us access to His promises, securing our firm foundation. Salvation is an important part of a firm foundation, so that you may receive the gift and benefit from its blessings in every arena of life. Faith is the foundation of living a victorious life as a Christian, and Jesus is the core of our existence and the basis of our firm foundation.

After you study the Word of God and apply its life-changing principles to your circumstances, you will see the Word works, and you will learn what it means to walk by faith and not by sight. You will know that the word of God is true and that it works. The Word of God has the ability to change our life situations, when we live, act according to, and do the Word. No matter where you are in life, the Word of the Lord can change that.

I pray that this book has served as a guide to lead you on a journey to success and prosperity in the things of God. You have been exposed to some of the basic teachings of Christianity. I believe you will receive continual direction in your walk with the Lord Jesus.

ABOUT THE AUTHOR

Apostle David A. Burgess was born and raised in St. Petersburg, Florida. In November 1998 at the age of twenty-eight, he joined the Lighthouse Ministries Discipleship Program in Riverview, Florida. Upon completion of a two-year course of rigorous teaching, he was called to a leadership role at Lighthouse Revival Center, where he served as an elder, associate pastor, and executive administrator for twelve years. There, he established the alumni Circle of the Rings, a tradition that is carried on to this day. He also coordinated the school of the prophetic at Lighthouse Revival Center. In 2012, he returned to south St. Petersburg to start a new work. He is the founder of Lighthouse Word of Faith Christian Center, where he serves as an apostle and senior pastor. Partnering with community organizations, he was able to establish one of the largest food banks in St. Petersburg, Florida. Along with that, he is greatly impacting and changing lives by teaching kingdom principles. Apostle David is a graduate from Faith Theological Seminary and Christian College

(FTSCC) of Tampa, Florida, where he received his master of ministry degree. He also established an affiliate campus of FTSCC in St. Petersburg, where he is a professor. In 2021, he established a church in Pakistan. He is a change agent for God!

Printed in the United States
by Baker & Taylor Publisher Services